# Jams & Jellies: Rid
## Recipes Anyone Can Make

by **Vesela Tabakova**
Text copyright(c)2014 Vesela Tabakova

**I Love You Mom!**

# Table Of Contents

# Is it Really So Simple?

When I think about my childhood I realize that growing up in a former Communist country was really interesting and very different from the way we live now. We usually had plenty of colorful fruit and vegetables in the summer but when winter came there was nothing particularly enticing in the food shops apart from basic food staples like meat, dairy and bread. No fresh fruit, no vegetables, no commercial sauces or ready-made meals - nothing for at least six or seven winter months until the next crops had grown and ripened. So everybody, and I mean literally every family, had one and the same ritual every summer – buying from the farmers` market or picking from our gardens fresh cherries, berries, peaches, plums, pears and seasonal vegetables like tomatoes, peppers, eggplants, green beans or peas and preparing different kinds of delicious preserves. All these summer fruits and vegetables, picked at their peak, when plentiful and prices are low, provided much needed variety when winter came. All the family members were involved in some way or another and it was fun but, more importantly, it was essential because it was the only way to ensure that we could eat a varied and healthy diet during the winter.

Now life has changed a lot and we no longer have to stock food for the colder months. There are plenty of fruit and vegetables available in the shops all year round and, of course, we now have freezers, too. But the tradition of canning and preserving the summer flavors in jars and filling the pantry with colorful jams, jellies and pickles to enjoy throughout the year has deep roots in our culture and we still do it. Moreover, summer vegetables and fruit have the highest nutritional content so preserving them for the cold months makes sense and is really not hard at all. Anyone can do it and it doesn't require much effort. Not only will you have preserved the best of the summer fruits for your own enjoyment, but you can give quite impressive gifts to friends that will be appreciated and long remembered.

Each summer my family prepares more than 200 jars of fruit preserves and pickled vegetables so we can use them all year long. As well as a great way to preserve the fresh, summer flavors this has the added benefit of giving us control over the quality of our food by avoiding any undesirable additives and preservatives found in many commercial products.

In my new series of recipe books I share my best homemade jams and jellies recipes and tips. If you are a veteran jam maker, you may find these recipes ridiculously easy. If, however, you are a novice, I believe you will actually enjoy making them and your family will certainly enjoy the taste of summer in the months ahead.

# Home Canning Requires Just a Few Basic Kitchen Tools and Knowledge of a Few Simple Principles:

- To prepare the healthiest and easiest jams in the world use just ripe, preferably organic, fruit and either organic sugar or organic honey. Using frozen or overripe fruit is not a good idea because they have lost their natural pectin. I don't add pectin to my jams and don't use sugar substitutes. The whole idea of jam-making is to preserve fruit with sugar so a sugar–free jam does not taste good and is not healthy at all because in order to make it you have to add some processed ingredients.

- The best jams can be easily made with just basic kitchen utensils - large, shallow pans, ladles and, of course, some jars with lids and rubber rings that create a vacuum seal. There is no need to use special canners or other equipment designed just for that purpose.

- Before filling the jars with the prepared jam you have to keep them hot either by simmering them together with the lids for at least 10 minutes or by keeping them in a 400 F-degree oven.

- Cook fruit very slowly at first over low heat to extract the maximum amount of juice and pectin. Stir frequently until tender, but do not overcook.

In Europe jam and jelly recipes usually call for equal amounts of sugar and fruit, by weight. Sugar acts as a preservative, so there is no need to add pectin. We just fill the jars with the hot jam and then turn them upside down. Once they've cooled, they are sealed and should last quite a few months. But if you prefer to follow the traditional way of sealing jam-filled jars, just place them into a large pot with a rack. Fill with water to cover the jars by at least 2 inches. Cover with a lid and bring to the boil. Boil for 10 minutes, remove the jars and set aside to cool. Bon Appetit!

## My Family's Jam and Jelly Recipes

One thing you always have to do before you start following the recipes is to wash your jars and lids in warm, soapy water or in the dishwasher. Then you place them in a large pot, with water to 2 inches above the jars, and boil them for 10 minutes. After that just leave the jars in hot water or in a warm oven until needed.

# Grandma's Strawberry Jam

## Makes 6-7 11 oz jars

## Ingredients:

4 lb fresh strawberries (stemmed and cleaned)

5 cups sugar

2 tbsp lemon juice or 1 tsp citric acid

## Directions:

Combine strawberries and sugar in a large, shallow saucepan and allow to stand for 3 to 4 hours or leave in the fridge overnight. Bring mixture slowly to the boil, stirring until sugar is dissolved. Boil for 40 minutes, skimming any foam off the top once or twice.

Drop a small amount of the jam on a plate and wait a minute to see if it has thickened. If it has gelled enough, turn off the heat. If not, keep boiling and test every 5 minutes until ready. Two or three minutes before you remove the jam from the heat, add lemon juice or citric acid and stir well.

Ladle the hot jam into the jars up to 1/8-inch from the top. Place the lid on top securely and flip the jar upside down. Continue until all of the jars are filled and upside down. Allow the jam to cool completely before turning right-side up. Press on the lid to check and see if it has sealed. If one of the jars' lids doesn't pop up, the jar is not sealed, so you should store it in the fridge.

My grandmother has been making jam for nearly 60 years and has never used a water bath. Her technique of turning the jars upside down creates a perfect seal and she has never had a failure. But if you decide to process the jams in the traditional way, place them into a large pot with a rack, cover the jars with water by at least 2 inches and bring to the boil. Boil for 10 minutes, remove the jars and allow to cool.

# A Different Strawberry Jam

**Makes 6-7 11 oz jars**

**Ingredients:**

4 lb fresh small strawberries (stemmed and cleaned)

5 cups sugar

1 cup water

2 tbsp lemon juice or 1 tsp citric acid

**Directions:**

Mix water and sugar and bring to the boil. Simmer sugar syrup for 5-6 minutes then slowly drop in the cleaned strawberries. Stir and bring to the boil again. Lower heat and simmer, stirring and skimming any foam off the top once or twice.

Drop a small amount of the jam on a plate and wait a minute to see if it has thickened. If it has gelled enough, turn off the heat. If not, keep boiling and test every 5 minutes until ready. Two or three minutes before you remove the jam from the heat, add lemon juice or citric acid and stir well.

Ladle the hot jam in the jars until 1/8-inch from the top. Place the lid on top and flip the jar upside down. Continue until all of the jars are filled and upside down.

Allow the jam to cool completely before turning right-side up. Press on the lid to check and see if it has sealed. If one of the jars lids doesn't pop up- the jar is not sealed–store it in a refrigerator.

# Raspberry Jam

**Makes 4-5 11 oz jars**

**Ingredients:**

4 cups raspberries

4 cups sugar

1 tsp vanilla extract

1/2 tsp citric acid

**Directions:**

Gently wash and drain the raspberries. Lightly crush them with a potato masher, food mill or a food processor. Do not puree, it is better to have bits of fruit. Sieve half of the raspberry pulp to remove some of the seeds. Combine sugar and raspberries in a wide, thick-bottomed pot and bring mixture to a full rolling boil, stirring constantly. Skim any scum or foam that rises to the surface. Boil until the jam sets.

Test by putting a small drop on a cold plate – if the jam is set, it will wrinkle when given a small poke with your finger. Add citric acid, vanilla, and stir. Simmer for 2-3 minutes more, then ladle into hot jars. Flip upside down or process 10 minutes in boiling water.

# Raspberry-Gooseberry Jam

**Makes 4-5 11 oz jars**

**Ingredients:**

2 cups raspberries

2 cups gooseberries

4 cups sugar

a pinch of salt

½ tsp citric acid

**Directions:**

Combine fruit and sugar in a wide saucepan. Stir and set aside for an hour. Gently boil fruit and sugar, stirring and removing any foam that rises to the surface. Boil until the jam sets.

Add citric acid, salt and stir. Simmer for 2-3 minutes more, then ladle into hot jars. Flip upside down or process 10 minutes in boiling water.

# Raspberry-Peach Jam

**Makes 4-5 11 oz jars**

**Ingredients:**

2 lb peaches

1 1/2 cup raspberries

4 cups sugar

1 tsp citric acid

**Directions:**

Wash and slice the peaches. Clean the raspberries and combine them with the peaches is a wide, heavy-bottomed saucepan. Cover with sugar and set aside for a few hours or overnight.

Bring the fruit and sugar to a boil over medium heat, stirring occasionally. Remove any foam that rises to the surface.

Boil until the jam sets. Add citric acid and stir. Simmer for 2-3 minutes more, then ladle into hot jars. Flip upside down or process 10 minutes in boiling water.

# Blueberry Jam

**Makes 4-5 11 oz jars**

**Ingredients:**

4 cups granulated sugar

3 cups blueberries (frozen and thawed or fresh)

3/4 cup honey

2 tbsp lemon juice

1 tsp lemon zest

**Directions:**

Gently wash and drain the blueberries. Lightly crush them with a potato masher, food mill or a food processor. Add the honey, lemon juice, and lemon zest, then bring to a boil over medium-high heat.

Boil for 10-15 minutes, stirring from time to time. Boil until the jam sets.

Test by putting a small drop on a cold plate – if the jam is set, it will wrinkle when given a small poke with your finger. Skim off any foam, then ladle the jam into jars. Seal, flip upside down or process for 10 minutes in boiling water.

# Triple Berry Jam

**Makes 4-5 11 oz jars**

**Ingredients:**

1 cup strawberries

1 cup raspberries

2 cups blueberries

4 cups sugar

1 tsp citric acid

**Directions:**

Mix berries and add sugar. Set aside for a few hours or overnight. Bring the fruit and sugar to the boil over medium heat, stirring frequently. Remove any foam that rises to the surface.

Boil until the jam sets. Add citric acid, salt and stir.

Simmer for 2-3 minutes more, then ladle into hot jars. Flip upside down or process 10 minutes in boiling water.

# Red Currant Jelly

**Makes 6-7 11 oz jars**

**Ingredients:**

2 lb fresh red currants

1/2 cup water

3 cups sugar

1 tsp citric acid

**Directions:**

Place the currants into a large pot, and crush with a potato masher or berry crusher. Add in water, and bring to a boil. Simmer for 10 minutes. Strain the fruit through a jelly or cheese cloth and measure out 4 cups of the juice.

Pour the juice into a large saucepan, and stir in the sugar. Bring to full rolling boil, then simmer for 20-30 minutes, removing any foam that may rise to the surface. When the jelly sets, ladle in hot jars, flip upside down or process in boiling water for 10 minutes.

# White Cherry Jam

**Makes 3-4 11 oz jars**

**Ingredients:**

2 lb cherries

3 cups sugar

2 cups water

1 tsp citric acid

**Directions:**

Wash and stone cherries. Combine water and sugar and bring to the boil.

Boil for 5-6 minutes then remove from heat and add cherries. Bring to a rolling boil and cook until set. Add citric acid, stir and boil 1-2 minutes more.

Ladle in hot jars, flip upside down or process in boiling water for 10 minutes.

# Cherry Jam

**Makes 3-4 11 oz jars**

**Ingredients:**

2 lb fresh cherries, pitted, halved

4 cups sugar

1/2 cup lemon juice

**Directions:**

Place the cherries in a large saucepan. Add sugar and set aside for an hour. Add the lemon juice and place over low heat. Cook, stirring occasionally, for 10 minutes or until sugar dissolves. Increase heat to high and bring to a rolling boil.

Cook for 5-6 minutes or until jam is set. Remove from heat and ladle hot jam into jars, seal and flip upside down.

# A Different Cherry Jam

**Makes 4-5 11 oz jars**

**Ingredients:**

2 lb cherries

3 cups sugar

2 cups water

1 tsp citric acid

**Directions:**

Wash and stone cherries. Combine water and sugar and bring to the boil. Boil for 5-6 minutes then remove from heat and add cherries. Bring to a rolling boil and cook until set. Add citric acid, stir and boil 1-2 minutes more.

Ladle in hot jars, flip upside down or process in boiling water for 10 minutes.

# Oven Baked Ripe Figs Jam

**Makes 3-4 11 oz jars**

**Ingredients:**

2 lb ripe figs

2 cups sugar

1 ½ cups water

2 tbsp lemon juice

**Directions:**

Arrange the figs in a Dutch oven, if they are very big, cut them in halves. Add sugar and water and stir well. Bake at 350 F for about one and a half hours. Do not stir.

You can check the readiness by dropping a drop of the syrup in a cup of cold water – if it falls to the bottom without dissolving, the jam is ready. If the drop dissolves before falling, you can bake it a little longer.

Take out of the oven, add lemon juice and ladle in the warm jars. Place the lids on top and flip the jars upside down. Allow the jam to cool completely before turning right-side up.

If you want to process the jams - place them into a large pot, cover the jars with water by at least 2 inches and bring to a boil. Boil for 10 minutes, remove the jars and sit to cool.

# Oven Baked Plum Jam

**Makes 5-6 11 oz jars**

**Ingredients:**

4 lb plums

3 cups sugar

1 cup water

1 tsp citric acid

a pinch of cinnamon

a pinch of ground cloves

**Directions:**

Halve the plums and take out the stones. Arrange them in a Dutch oven and cover with sugar. Add in water and bake at 350 F for 2 hours. Add citric acid and spices, ladle in hot jars and flip upside down.

If you want to process the jams - place them into a large pot, covers the jars with water by at least 2 inches and bring to a boil. Boil for 10 minutes, remove the jars and sit to cool.

# Quince Jam

**Makes 5-6 11 oz jars**

**Ingredients:**

4 lb quinces

5 cups sugar

2 cups water

1 tsp lemon zest

3 tbsp lemon juice

**Directions:**

Combine water and sugar in a deep, thick-bottomed saucepan and bring it to the boil. Simmer, stirring until the sugar has completely dissolved. Rinse the quinces, cut in half, and discard the cores. Grate the quinces, using a cheese grater or a blender to make it faster. Quince flesh tends to darken very quickly, so it is good to do this as fast as possible.

Add the grated quinces to the sugar syrup and cook uncovered, stirring occasionally until the jam turns pink and thickens to desired consistency, about 40 minutes.

Drop a small amount of the jam on a plate and wait a minute to see if it has thickened. If it has gelled enough, turn off the heat. If not, keep boiling and test every 2-3 minutes until ready. Two or three minutes before you remove the jam from the heat, add lemon juice and lemon zest and stir well.

Ladle in hot, sterilized jars and flip upside down.

# Quince Jelly

**Makes 5-6 11 oz jars**

**Ingredients:**

3 lbs quinces

about 4 cups sugar (enough to add a cup of sugar for every cup of juice)

6 cups of water

½ tsp citric acid

**Directions:**

Wash and cut the quinces, but do not peel them and keep the cores too. Put the quinces in a deep, heavy-bottomed pot and cover with water. Bring to the boil and simmer for 30 minutes.

Strain the quince juice and measure it. It should be about 4 cups. Pour it in the pot again and bring to a boil. Add the sugar - a little less than a cup for every cup of juice. Stir until the sugar dissolves, then simmer, skimming any foam off the top in necessary.

Cook the quince jelly until when you drop a small amount of it on a plate after a minute it has thickened. Add the citric acid, simmer for 2-3 minutes more and remove from the stove. Ladle in hot jars, and flip upside down.

# Quince and Apple Jam

**Makes 5-6 11 oz jars**

**Ingredients:**

2 medium quinces, peeled and diced

3 large apples, diced

3 cups sugar

2 cups water

½ cup lemon juice

**Directions:**

Place the quinces, lemon juice, sugar, and water in a saucepan and bring to the boil. Simmer for 10 minutes, then add in the apples. Simmer for 10 more minutes, or until the jam is set.

Ladle into the warm, sterilized jars and seal. Flip upside down or process in boiling water for 10 minutes.

# Apple Jam

**Makes 4-5 11 oz jars**

**Ingredients:**

2 lb apples, washed

4 cups sugar

½ tsp cinnamon

2 tsp lemon juice or 1/2 teaspoon citric acid

**Directions:**

Slice the apples and place in a large, thick bottomed saucepan. Cover with the sugar, add in lemon juice and cinnamon and bring to the boil stirring continuously.

Boil for 30 minutes, removing any foam that may rise to the surface. When the jam sets, ladle in hot jars, flip upside down or process in boiling water for 10 minutes.

# Apple and Blackberry Jam

**Makes 5-6 11 oz jars**

**Ingredients:**

2 lb blackberries

2 big apples, cut in cubes

5 cups sugar

4 tbsp lemon juice

**Directions:**

Place the blackberries and the apples in a saucepan and cover with the lemon juice and sugar. Set aside for an hour. Bring to the boil, then reduce the heat and simmer until set.

Remove from heat, add citric acid and stir. Boil for 2-3 minutes more and ladle into hot jars. Flip upside down or process 10 minutes in boiling water.

# Aromatic Pear Jam

**Makes 4-5 11 oz jars**

**Ingredients:**

6 medium pears, diced

4 cups sugar

½ cup lemon juice

½ tsp cloves

**Directions:**

Combine fruit, sugar, lemon juice and spice and bring to the boil, stirring constantly until sugar is dissolved.

Boil until jam is set. Ladle into hot jars and flip upside down or process 10 minutes in boiling water.

# Pear and Apple Jam

**Makes 4-5 11 oz jars**

**Ingredients:**

2 big apples, diced

4 medium pears, diced

4 cups sugar

½ cup lemon juice

½ tsp cloves

**Directions:**

Combine fruit, sugar and lemon juice and spice and bring to the boil, stirring constantly until sugar is dissolved.

Boil until jam is thick. Ladle into hot jars and flip upside down or process 10 minutes in boiling water.

# Peach Jam

**Makes 6-7 11 oz jars**

**Ingredients:**

4 lb peaches, peeled, pitted and sliced

6 cups sugar

2 tbsp lemon juice

**Directions:**

Slice the peaches and combine them with sugar in a large pot. Bring to a boil, stirring gently, then lower heat to medium and simmer for 30 minutes, stirring constantly.

Test if the jam is set by putting a small drop on a cold plate – it is set if it wrinkles when given a small poke with your finger. Skim any foam, add lemon juice and stir. Simmer for 2-3 minutes more, then ladle into hot jars. Flip upside down or process 10 minutes in boiling water.

# Apricot Vanilla Jam

**Makes 4-5 11 oz jars**

**Ingredients:**

2 lb apricots, coarsely chopped

3 cups sugar

1 tsp vanilla extract

2 tbsp lemon juice

**Directions:**

Wash, stone and chop the apricots. Put them in a wide saucepan. Crack 6-7 of the stones and put the kernels in the saucepan too. Add sugar and stir. Bring gently to the boil and cook, stirring frequently, until thickened.

Add vanilla and the lemon juice, stir and boil for a minute more. Carefully ladle into hot jars. Seal, flip upside down or process for 10 minutes in boiling water.

# Apricot Jelly

**Makes 5-6 11 oz jars**

**Ingredients:**

2 lbs apricots

about 3 cups sugar (enough to add a cup of sugar for every cup of juice)

2 cups apple juice

½ tsp citric acid

**Directions:**

Wash, stone and chop the apricots. Put then in a deep, heavy-bottomed pot and cover with water. Bring to the boil and simmer for 30 minutes. Sieve the apricots and strain juice from pulp then and measure it. Pour the apricot juice in the pot again and bring to a boil.

Add the sugar - a little less than a cup for every cup of juice. Add in the apple juice. Stir until the sugar dissolves, then simmer, skimming any foam off the top in necessary.

Cook the apricot jelly until when you drop a small amount of it on a plate after a minute it has thickened. Add the citric acid, simmer for 2-3 minutes more and remove from the stove. Ladle in hot jars, and flip upside down.

# Pumpkin Jam

**Makes 6-7 11 oz jars**

**Ingredients:**

2 lb pumpkin, cut in cubes

1 cup dried apricots, chopped

1 cup raisins

3 cups sugar

1 tsp citric acid

**Directions:**

Cut the pumpkin and put it in a wide saucepan. Cover with sugar, stir and leave overnight or for a few hours.

Add apricots and raisins. Slowly bring to the boil, then simmer, stirring frequently, until the pumpkin is tender.

Add citric acid, boil for a few minutes more and gently ladle in jars. Flip upside down or process for 10 minutes in boiling water.

# Caramelized Onion Jam

**Makes 3-4 11 oz jars**

**Ingredients:**

1.3 lb red onions, thinly sliced

½ cup water

1 tbsp olive oil

1 spring fresh thyme

2 tbsp brown sugar

2 tbsp balsamic vinegar

**Directions:**

Heat olive oil in a saucepan over medium heat. Add onions and thyme. Cook, stirring occasionally, for 15-20 minutes or until golden. Add sugar and continue cooking for 3 minutes. Add in vinegar and 1/2 cup cold water.

Bring to the boil, reduce heat to low and simmer, uncovered, for 5 minutes or until thick. Ladle in hot jars, flip upside down or process in boiling water for 10 minutes.

## About the Author

I live in Bulgaria with my family of six (including the Jack Russell Terrier). My passion is going green in everyday life and I prepare homemade cosmetic and beauty products for all my family and friends.

My recently discovered enthusiasm for writing will bring you more interesting cookbooks as well as natural and green beauty recipe books.

If you want to see other cookbooks that I have published, together with some natural beauty books, you can check out my Author Page on Amazon.

Thank you very much for downloading my book!

Vesela Tabakova

Made in the USA
Columbia, SC
22 April 2020